Strongholds
Breaking the Radicalization
of
Right and Left
America

A PAMPHLET INITIATIVE OF

The
Freeman
Institute
FOR INTEGRATIVE RESEARCH

By Eric J. Freeman, PhD

A PAMPHLET INITIATIVE OF

The
Freeman
Institute

FOR INTEGRATIVE RESEARCH

Published by
The Freeman Institute for Integrative Research
201 Columbia Mall Blvd.
Columbia, SC 29223

ISBN 979-8-218-62302-9

First Edition

Note on Public Domain Materials

The text of *Mein Kampf* has been in the public domain in various countries due to the passage of time and legal rulings. The references to this work in this handbook are made solely for educational and analytical purposes, in accordance with fair use principles. The intent is to examine historical patterns of radicalization and propaganda to better understand the ideological forces shaping the present. This handbook does not endorse any of the views expressed in *Mein Kampf*, nor does it seek to promote or disseminate its ideology.

The Freeman Institute for Integrative Research

This instrument is a product of *The Pamphlet Initiative* of The Freeman Institute for Integrative Research, an interdisciplinary entity dedicated to examining complex societal issues through multiple academic lenses. The Institute focuses particularly on political polarization, ideological extremism, and the historical context of social divisions that contribute to a more comprehensive understanding of America's current civic landscape.

Through *The Pamphlet Initiative*, the Institute develops accessible, research-informed resources that bridge theoretical scholarship with practical application. This pamphlet on ideological radicalization exemplifies the Institute's commitment to integrating political science, historical analysis, and social psychology to provide civic leaders, educators, and concerned citizens with frameworks that foster both intellectual honesty and constructive dialogue across America's deepening political divides.

Table of Contents

PREFACE

America stands at a crossroads. The polarization that defines our era is no longer just a matter of differing opinions—it has become a culture of ideological warfare, where both the radical right and radical left engage in tactics that mirror each other in striking ways. It is within this turbulent landscape that *Strongholds! Breaking the Radicalization of Right & Left America* emerges as a crucial guide.

My background in orthodox social ethics, homiletics, and history has shaped my understanding of how societies succumb to ideological extremes. My work has consistently centered on understanding historical patterns of radicalization and how they manifest in contemporary discourse. This handbook is not just an academic exercise—it is a call to action for those who wish to navigate political and social landscapes with clarity, nuance, and intellectual honesty.

This guide is not about demonizing any one ideology but about understanding how radicalization happens on both sides. Whether it is the rhetoric of "internal enemies" on the right or the institutionally enforced moral exceptionalism on the left, the mechanisms remain the same. We must ask ourselves: Has my perspective been shaped by radicalization? Have I unknowingly contributed to the cycle of ideological rigidity, demonization, and exclusion?

Understanding radicalization requires confronting difficult historical precedents. A critical component of this analysis is *Mein Kampf*—one of history's most infamous texts. While referencing Adolf Hitler's work is painful, it remains one of the most explicit historical blueprints of how authoritarian rhetoric, manipulation, and propaganda operate. This handbook does not endorse or legitimize Hitler's ideology; rather, it dissects the patterns of radicalization, propaganda, and dehumanization that persist today in both right-wing and left-wing extremism. By studying this text in context, we gain invaluable insights into how extremist movements justify their actions and how societies can resist falling into their traps.

However, we must also recognize the limitations of using *Mein Kampf* as a contemporary reference point. The conditions that birthed Nazi Germany are vastly different from the present, and modern radicalization operates within new frameworks—particularly through social media, mass communication, and institutional influence. This guide uses *Mein Kampf* not as a direct comparison but as a historical case study—a lens through which we can identify recurring patterns of extremism and challenge their presence in today's America.

As you engage with this guide, I encourage you to reflect critically on your own perspectives. Have you uncritically accepted simplistic narratives? Do you find yourself drawn to sources that only confirm your preexisting beliefs? Are you willing to engage with differing perspectives, or do you dismiss them as inherently evil? These are difficult but necessary questions, and this handbook exists to challenge—not comfort—those who are truly committed to intellectual and ethical integrity.

Ultimately, this is an invitation. Just as the little boy in Hans Christian Andersen's *The Emperor's New Clothes* had the courage to acknowledge the obvious, deradicalization requires each of us—our own emperors in this hyper-individualistic culture—to realize that we are, in fact, bare. It is not wrongheaded to recognize the truth when the evidence is clear, nor is it weakness to admit we have been deceived by illusions of ideological purity. An invitation to resist the allure of radicalism, to think beyond tribal allegiances, and to engage with ideas in a way that promotes democracy, civil discourse, and human dignity. History has shown us where unchallenged extremism leads—our responsibility is to ensure that we do not repeat its mistakes. After nearly four decades as a Christian cleric, I recognize that these radical factions are but manifestations of a deeper battle, one not merely of flesh and blood, but of *spiritual wickedness in high places*, as described in the Apostle Paul's letter to the Ephesians. The forces that drive extremism, division, and deception are not new, nor can they be dismantled by political or intellectual means alone. We must be willing to confront the deeper, unseen forces that influence human affairs.

1

WHY *MEIN KAMPF* MATTERS AS A HISTORICAL REFERENCE

In the study of radicalization, few texts are as instructive—yet as deeply troubling—as *Mein Kampf.* Written by Adolf Hitler in the 1920s, this work provides a firsthand account of how extremist ideologies are formed, how they justify violence, and how they exploit societal divisions to gain power.

This chapter does not seek to glorify or lend credibility to Hitler's ideology; rather, it aims to highlight *Mein Kampf* as a historical document that offers critical insights into how totalitarian rhetoric can be used to manipulate public sentiment. Understanding how these rhetorical strategies function is essential if we hope to recognize and resist similar patterns in today's world.

The Power of Propaganda and Emotional Manipulation

One of the most striking features of *Mein Kampf* is Hitler's understanding of mass psychology. He recognized that propaganda works best when it is simple, repetitive, and emotionally charged. He wrote:

> *"All effective propaganda must be confined to a few points and must harp on these slogans."*

Modern parallels to this principle are easy to find. Political messaging today—whether from mainstream media, political campaigns, or social movements—often follows the same pattern. Slogans and emotionally charged phrases dominate the discourse, leaving little room for nuance or deeper reflection.

A Blueprint for Authoritarianism

Beyond propaganda, *Mein Kampf* provides a playbook for how authoritarian regimes justify their actions. It emphasizes:

- The identification of enemies as a unifying force
- The demonization of dissenters
- The perpetuation of victimhood as a justification for aggressive action

These strategies are not unique to Nazi Germany; they have appeared in various authoritarian movements throughout history. When political leaders or groups frame themselves as perpetual victims and justify extreme actions in the name of self-defense, it is crucial to recognize the historical precedent.

Recurring Ideological Strategies in the Present

While the world today is vastly different from the 1920s, the rhetorical devices and manipulative tactics outlined in *Mein Kampf* still find resonance in modern political discourse. Consider the following passage:

"The great masses of people will more easily fall victims to a big lie than to a small one."

This concept of the "big lie" remains relevant in an era of widespread misinformation. Both ends of the political spectrum have weaponized half-truths and distortions to shape public opinion, often relying on emotionally charged narratives that obscure complexity in favor of simple, convenient explanations.

Why This Matters Now

Understanding *Mein Kampf* as a historical reference does not mean equating current events directly with Nazi Germany. However, it does mean acknowledging that radicalization follows patterns—patterns that can be recognized and countered. If we fail to learn from history, we risk repeating its mistakes.

This chapter serves as a foundation for the rest of this guidebook. By studying how propaganda, victimhood narratives, and authoritarian rhetoric function, we equip ourselves to critically assess the political messages we consume. In doing so, we take the first step toward resisting ideological manipulation and preserving civil discourse.

2

ACKNOWLEDGING THE SENSITIVITY OF THIS ANALYSIS

Discussing *Mein Kampf* is inherently difficult. The text is widely regarded as one of the most dangerous works in modern history, having laid the ideological groundwork for a regime responsible for mass genocide and the most devastating global conflict of the 20th century. For many, simply engaging with its content can evoke deep pain, anger, and fear. This chapter acknowledges that sensitivity and seeks to clarify why examining this text critically is necessary.

Why This Discussion is Necessary

Some may question whether it is even appropriate to analyze *Mein Kampf* in a modern context. However, history shows that ignoring the tactics of extremism does not make them disappear; rather, it can allow them to flourish unchecked. By engaging with this text, we are not legitimizing it, but rather dismantling its manipulative strategies and identifying how similar rhetoric is used today.

A Painful but Critical Study

The trauma inflicted by Hitler's ideology remains fresh in the collective memory of many. Holocaust survivors and their descendants, as well as those whose families were affected by World War II, may find any reference to *Mein Kampf* unsettling. However, understanding how its ideas took hold allows us to recognize when similar patterns arise.

A crucial passage from *Mein Kampf* illustrates the calculated nature of propaganda:

> *"The receptivity of the masses is very limited, their intelligence is small, but their power of forgetting is enormous. In consequence of these facts, all effective propaganda must be confined to a few points and must harp on these in slogans."*

This manipulative principle is not confined to the past. Modern extremist movements employ similar methods, using social media, soundbites, and slogans to push oversimplified narratives and stoke division. Acknowledging this does not diminish the pain of history—it strengthens our resistance to the repetition of these tactics.

The Ethical Responsibility of Examining Historical Extremism

We must be clear: studying *Mein Kampf* does not mean endorsing it. On the contrary, failing to study its rhetorical devices leaves us vulnerable to their resurgence in contemporary society. This handbook approaches the text with caution, ensuring that our engagement is always through a lens of **historical awareness, ethical responsibility, and an unwavering commitment to opposing extremism in all its forms.**

Navigating Emotional Responses

It is understandable to feel discomfort when engaging with a text that represents such profound human suffering. However, rather than avoiding difficult history, we must confront it. When approached critically, *Mein Kampf* is not just a relic of the past but a warning against the dangers of unexamined ideology.

As we move forward, we do so with a deep respect for those affected by Hitler's atrocities and with a steadfast commitment to ensuring that history's darkest moments are never repeated.

THE LIMITS OF APPLYING *MEIN KAMPF* TO MODERN SOCIETY

While *Mein Kampf* provides valuable insights into extremist rhetoric, it is important to recognize its limitations when analyzing contemporary political movements. The world today differs significantly from the historical conditions that allowed Nazi ideology to take root. This chapter explores the contextual differences that make direct comparisons problematic, while also acknowledging the recurring patterns that remain relevant.

Historical Context Matters

Nazi Germany was shaped by unique historical circumstances—economic devastation following World War I, deep national humiliation, and a lack of democratic tradition. Hitler capitalized on these conditions to consolidate power, presenting himself as the savior of a nation in crisis. While modern societies face their own challenges, they do so within different economic, social, and institutional frameworks.

We must be cautious when drawing parallels between past and present. Overgeneralized comparisons can distort our understanding of current threats, leading to misguided responses rather than effective solutions.

Modern Technology Has Changed Propaganda

In Hitler's time, propaganda was primarily disseminated through print, radio, and public speeches. The rise of digital media has fundamentally changed the way information spreads. Today, disinformation and extremist rhetoric can reach global audiences instantly, bypassing traditional gatekeepers such as editors and fact-checkers.

Algorithms amplify content based on engagement rather than accuracy, making ideological echo chambers more pervasive than ever. This shift means that while the tactics of persuasion outlined in *Mein Kampf* remain relevant, they must be understood in the context of modern communication technology.

Political Movements Are More Complex Than in the 1930s

The Nazi movement was characterized by rigid hierarchical control, state-sponsored propaganda, and a singular authoritarian leader. Modern political extremism, whether on the right or left, often operates in more decentralized ways. Grassroots movements, online activism, and loosely affiliated groups complicate the traditional understanding of ideological radicalization.

Additionally, modern democracies have stronger institutional safeguards against authoritarian takeovers.

While these safeguards are not infallible, they provide critical checks and balances that did not exist in Weimar Germany.

Recognizing Recurring Extremist Strategies Without Overstating Parallels

While the exact conditions of Nazi Germany are unlikely to repeat, *Mein Kampf* remains a valuable case study in identifying the mechanisms of radicalization. Understanding how authoritarian rhetoric, scapegoating, and victimhood narratives function can help us recognize when these tactics appear in contemporary discourse.

However, applying *Mein Kampf* too literally to modern politics risks oversimplifying complex issues. Instead, we should use it as a tool for critical analysis, ensuring that we remain vigilant without resorting to alarmist comparisons.

By engaging with history thoughtfully, we can learn from the past while avoiding the pitfalls of misapplying historical lessons to the present.

RECOGNIZING THE PATTERNS OF
RADICALIZATION

Radicalization is not a spontaneous occurrence. It follows a **predictable trajectory**, often fueled by **fear, resentment, and a sense of injustice**. While ideological movements differ in their specific goals, the strategies they use to recruit followers and sustain their influence share **remarkable similarities**. This chapter will explore the **common patterns of radicalization**, showing how these tactics have been used throughout history and how they manifest today.

Demonization of Opponents

One of the earliest steps in radicalization is the identification of an enemy. Political or ideological groups rely on demonizing opponents to create a clear "us vs. them" dynamic. By framing a specific group as a threat to society, radical movements unite their followers under a common cause.

In *Mein Kampf,* Hitler wrote:

> *"The broad masses of a population are more amenable to the appeal of rhetoric than to any other force."*

Modern parallels to this tactic can be found in both right-wing and left-wing movements. Whether it is the labeling of political adversaries as "traitors" or "oppressors," the intent is the same—to make dialogue and cooperation impossible by turning disagreement into moral failing.

Dehumanization as Justification

After identifying an enemy, the next step in radicalization is to **strip that enemy of their humanity**. This stage is essential, as it allows individuals to justify violence, suppression, or exclusion.

A well-known concept in propaganda is the enemy as a subhuman force, unworthy of respect or engagement. Dehumanization often manifests in:

- Stereotyping opponents with exaggerated and negative traits.
- Using language that compares people to animals, diseases, or inanimate threats.
- Dismissing entire groups as irredeemable or beyond reform.

Once people are successfully dehumanized, hateful rhetoric and violent actions become more acceptable to the general public.

Exaggerated Rhetoric and Propaganda

Radical movements thrive on emotionally charged language. They employ simplified slogans, half-truths, and dramatic narratives to evoke strong emotional reactions. Hitler's propaganda relied on grandiose promises and fearmongering, tactics that still resonate in modern political discourse.

In *Mein Kampf,* he wrote:

"The most brilliant propagandist technique will yield no success unless one fundamental principle is borne in mind constantly—it must confine itself to a few points and repeat them over and over."

This is evident today in social media echo chambers, political campaigns, and extremist rhetoric, where complex issues are reduced to easily digestible talking points that discourage deeper inquiry.

Selective Interpretation of Decline

Radicalization often involves exploiting a real or perceived decline in society. This decline is framed as being caused by a **b** while ignoring other contributing factors.

This pattern is visible in:

- Economic instability being blamed solely on a political ideology or group.
- Cultural changes framed as an orchestrated attack on tradition.
- Institutions portrayed as irredeemably corrupt, requiring complete dismantling rather than reform.

By focusing on a singular narrative, radical movements prevent their followers from considering alternative explanations or engaging in **constructive** problem-solving.

Conclusion: Recognizing These Patterns in Ourselves

It is easy to recognize these tactics in historical authoritarian regimes or political opponents, but it is far more challenging to identify them in our own beliefs and behaviors. Radicalization is not limited to extremists on the fringes—it can influence mainstream political discourse, media narratives, and even personal conversations.

To counter radicalization, we must cultivate critical thinking, self-awareness, and intellectual humility. The following chapters will focus on how radicalization affects both the right and the left, and what can be done to break free from these ideological strongholds.

HOW RADICALIZATION HAPPENS ON BOTH SIDES

Radicalization is not exclusive to any one ideology. It manifests across the political spectrum, using different narratives but employing remarkably similar tactics. Understanding these mechanisms is crucial in identifying how individuals and groups become entrenched in extreme worldviews and how society can work toward deradicalization.

The Radical Right: The Search for Internal Enemies

One of the defining characteristics of right-wing radicalization is the belief in internal subversion—the idea that the nation or culture is under attack from within. This often results in identifying "enemies of the people" who must be exposed and neutralized. Common targets include:

- Political elites accused of corruption or betrayal.
- Globalist forces blamed for undermining national sovereignty.
- Minority groups perceived as threats to traditional values or economic stability.

This narrative is reinforced through conspiracy theories, selective historical interpretations, and emotional appeals to patriotism and nostalgia. The goal is to foster a siege mentality, convincing adherents that their way of life is at existential risk.

The Radical Left: The Singular Focus on Systemic Oppression

Left-wing radicalization, while often advocating for equity and justice, can take on extreme forms that mirror authoritarian tendencies. A defining feature is the perception that all societal problems stem from systemic oppression. Common targets include:

- Capitalist structures seen as inherently exploitative.
- Law enforcement and institutions viewed as tools of repression.
- Opponents accused of perpetuating racism, sexism, or other forms of discrimination.

The radical left often promotes a moral absolutism that rejects nuance, painting dissenters as complicit in oppression. Cancel culture and ideological purity tests serve to reinforce group loyalty while silencing opposition, ensuring that the movement remains ideologically rigid.

Shared Mechanisms of Radicalization

Despite their ideological differences, both extremes rely on similar mechanisms to cultivate radicalization. These include:

1. **Us vs. Them Thinking** – Defining a clear enemy consolidates group identity and justifies extreme measures.
2. **Echo Chambers** – Information is curated to confirm biases, eliminating dissenting views.
3. **Demonization of Opponents** – Disagreement is framed as betrayal or moral failing.
4. **Justification of Aggressive Tactics** – Violence, censorship, or coercion is seen as necessary to achieve ideological purity.
5. **Emotional Manipulation** – Fear, anger, and outrage drive engagement and loyalty.

Breaking the Cycle

To prevent radicalization, individuals and societies must:

- Recognize ideological manipulation by critically assessing media and political rhetoric.
- Engage with differing perspectives instead of isolating oneself in echo chambers.
- Emphasize complexity over simplicity, acknowledging that social issues have multiple contributing factors.
- Promote civil discourse, even with those holding opposing views.

Radicalization thrives in environments of division and distrust. Understanding how it happens on both sides is essential to countering its spread and fostering a more informed, engaged, and united society.

A SOLUTION-ORIENTED PERSPECTIVE

Understanding radicalization is only the first step. The real challenge lies in addressing it effectively, both at the societal and individual levels. The solutions to radicalization are neither simple nor immediate, but they begin with personal accountability and a commitment to engaging with ideas critically and honestly.

Recognizing Our Own Biases

One of the most difficult yet crucial steps in resisting radicalization is acknowledging our own ideological biases. Everyone has them, but when left unchecked, biases can lead us into echo chambers where only confirming perspectives are heard, reinforcing division and hostility.

Ask yourself:

- Do I label entire groups as "the problem" without considering nuance and complexity?
- Do I engage with opposing viewpoints, or do I dismiss them as inherently evil or misguided?
- Have I justified extreme actions against perceived enemies, even in the name of justice?

Radicalization thrives in environments where people refuse to self-examine. By developing intellectual humility, we create space for dialogue and understanding.

Embracing Complex Thought

The world is rarely black and white. Political, social, and economic issues are complex, and simplistic explanations often do more harm than good. Avoiding radicalization means resisting the temptation to adopt one-size-fits-all narratives that reduce entire groups of people to villains or heroes.

- Seek out diverse sources of information, including those that challenge your preexisting beliefs.
- Ask critical questions rather than accept information at face value.
- Recognize that uncertainty is part of being an informed citizen—certainty in ideological extremes often signals indoctrination, not knowledge.

Breaking Free from Echo Chambers

Social media and modern news consumption habits have created ideological silos where people only interact with content that aligns with their beliefs. Escaping this cycle requires intentional effort:

- Follow and read sources across the political spectrum.
- Engage in meaningful conversations with those who hold different views.
- Resist the urge to unfollow, block, or "cancel" people simply because they disagree with you.

Rebuilding Civil Discourse

Democracy and social harmony depend on our ability to engage in respectful discourse. We must prioritize listening over reacting, even when confronted with views that challenge us. Civil discourse involves:

- Approaching discussions with curiosity instead of hostility.
- Distinguishing between disagreeing and dehumanizing.
- Encouraging open debate without resorting to personal attacks.

Actionable Steps for Change

1. **Seek Understanding Before Judgment** – Before dismissing someone's perspective, try to understand where they are coming from.
2. **Prioritize Facts Over Feelings** – Emotional responses are natural, but they should not override evidence-based reasoning.
3. **Promote Media Literacy** – Learn to recognize propaganda, misinformation, and manipulative rhetoric.
4. **Model the Behavior You Want to See** – Be the example of respectful engagement and critical thinking in your communities.
5. **Encourage Institutional Accountability** – Call for responsible reporting, ethical leadership, and transparency in governance.

Final Call to Action

The lessons of *Mein Kampf* are not confined to history—they are warnings for the present. Radicalization begins when we stop seeing people as individuals and start seeing them only as ideological representations.

To preserve democracy and civil discourse, we must:

- Resist emotional manipulation.
- Reject simplistic narratives.
- Engage critically, even with our own side.

This handbook is an invitation to reflect, challenge assumptions, and resist extremism in all its forms. True change begins when individuals take responsibility for their own thinking and commit to a more informed, compassionate, and balanced approach to discourse.

EPILOGUE

Chapter-by-Chapter Summary of *Mein Kampf* with Key Themes Related to the Current American Geopolitical Landscape

A Summary Analysis

Chapter 1: In the Home of My Parents

- **Summary:** Hitler recounts his childhood, family background, and early exposure to German nationalism. He expresses his belief in the necessity of uniting all German-speaking peoples.

- **Key Themes:** National identity and cultural cohesion.

- **Modern Parallels:** National identity discourse in the U.S., particularly around immigration and cultural homogenization.

- **Similar Tactics Across Extremes:** The extreme right pushes ethnic nationalism and "America First" rhetoric, while the extreme left defines national identity through an institutionally directed global citizenry. This is radical because it is not an organic evolution of the nation but a manufactured imposition of national identity, moving beyond civil rights of the oppressed to idealistic redefinitions by a narrow group of ideologues. Each side promotes a form of radical nationalism—one based on "America First," the other on "Moral Exceptionalism," where the U.S. is positioned as a global enforcer of ideological values. Demonization of opponents as either "unpatriotic" or "bigoted" leads to dehumanization, making reconciliation difficult.

Chapter 2: Years of Study and Suffering in Vienna

- **Summary:** Hitler details his years of struggle in Vienna, his growing anti-Semitic views, and his exposure to Marxism and class struggles.

- **Key Themes:** Economic hardship, radicalization through adversity, scapegoating minorities.

- **Modern Parallels:** Economic anxieties fueling populist movements in the U.S.

- **Similar Tactics Across Extremes:** The extreme right blames immigrants and minorities for economic instability, while the extreme left blames capitalism and the wealthy, both oversimplifying economic issues to rally support. By framing their targets as responsible for suffering, both sides justify their dehumanization and eventual exclusion.

Chapter 3: General Political Considerations Based on My Vienna Period

- **Summary:** Hitler criticizes the Austro-Hungarian Empire, arguing that multiculturalism weakens national unity. He outlines his early thoughts on political manipulation and propaganda.

- **Key Themes:** Multiculturalism vs. nationalism, media influence.

- **Modern Parallels:** Debates on immigration and multicultural policies in the U.S.

- **Similar Tactics Across Extremes:** The extreme right opposes immigration and cultural diversity, while the extreme left imposes an orchestrated national identity based on a controlled globalist vision rather than an organic national consensus. This redefinition is not based on broad democratic agreement but on institutional enforcement, where dissenting views are labeled regressive. Each side labels dissenters as "traitors" or "oppressors," fostering division and justifying punitive measures.

Chapter 4: Munich

- **Summary:** Hitler moves to Munich and finds an ideological home in German nationalism. He

begins associating with political groups that
oppose democracy and socialism.

- **Key Themes:** Political radicalization, anti-
democratic sentiments.

- **Modern Parallels:** The rise of extremism and
distrust in democratic institutions in the U.S.

- **Similar Tactics Across Extremes:** The extreme
right seeks to dismantle democratic norms under
the guise of national security, while the extreme
left often demonizes those who disagree with their
approach to resolving systemic oppression,
typically through intimated intellectual superiority.
This demonization facilitates dehumanization,
justifying exclusion or suppression.

Chapter 5: The War Years

- **Summary:** Hitler discusses his experience as a
soldier in World War I and how he became
disillusioned with Germany's defeat, which he
attributes to betrayal rather than military failure.

- **Key Themes:** National trauma, blame-shifting for
national decline.

- **Modern Parallels:** "Stolen election" narratives
and historical revisionism.

- **Similar Tactics Across Extremes:** The extreme
right selectively sees "internal enemies" such as

the deep state and globalists but fails to acknowledge systemic oppression. Meanwhile, the extreme left selectively sees systemic oppression as the primary source of national decline while overlooking social structure experimentations and oligarchy-like power plays as punitive measures against those who do not align with their ideals. Both sides vilify opponents, making their destruction—whether political, social, or institutional—appear justified.

Chapter 6: War Propaganda

- **Summary:** Hitler argues that propaganda should be simple, repetitive, and emotionally charged. He critiques German propaganda during WWI and praises British tactics.

- **Key Themes:** Propaganda's role in shaping national attitudes.

- **Modern Parallels:** The use of media and misinformation in shaping political narratives.

- **Similar Tactics Across Extremes:** The extreme right employs conspiracy theories and nationalist propaganda, while the extreme left frames dissent as dangerous regressivism. Both use media narratives to remove nuance and justify treating opponents as existential threats.

Chapter 7: The Revolution

- **Summary:** Hitler describes the collapse of the German Empire and the rise of the Weimar Republic, which he blames on Jews and socialists.

- **Key Themes:** Fear of national decline, scapegoating, rejection of democracy.

- **Modern Parallels:** Demonization of political opponents.

- **Similar Tactics Across Extremes:** The extreme right targets immigrants, progressives, and globalists, while the extreme left targets conservatives, capitalists, and traditional institutions. Once labeled as "traitors" or "fascists," dehumanization follows, justifying their suppression.

Final Thoughts

- *Mein Kampf* provides a historical case study in authoritarian rhetoric, propaganda, and nationalist extremism.

- **Lessons for the U.S.:** The dangers of misinformation, scapegoating, and extreme partisanship.

- **Relevance Today:** Both the extreme right and extreme left use similar tactics—whether through racial or intellectual superiority narratives—to divide society and consolidate power. Their approaches differ in rhetoric but share fundamental strategies: identifying an "enemy," suppressing dissent, and radicalizing supporters to justify increasingly extreme measures. This cycle follows the pattern: Demonize, Dehumanize, Destroy.

- **Radical Nationalism on Both Extremes:** The extreme right promotes "America First" as a form of exclusionary nationalism, while the extreme left advances a manufactured and institutionally imposed national identity that moves beyond civil rights to idealistic redefinitions by a narrow group of ideologues. Unlike natural democratic shifts in identity, this imposition relies on institutional mechanisms to enforce a specific vision, marginalizing dissent. Both perspectives fuel polarization and justify extreme actions against those who oppose their vision.

APPENDIX I

Christian Workbook

Strongholds! Breaking the Radicalization of Right & Left America

A Reflection & Devotional Guide

In a time when division and polarization dominate our culture, we must turn to scripture for wisdom, discernment, and healing. Radicalization—whether on the right or the left—often thrives on fear, misinformation, and the rejection of truth. As Christians, we are called to pursue truth, peace, and justice in all circumstances. This workbook is designed to help you reflect on these themes, guided by biblical principles, prayer, and self-examination.

Week 1: The Battle for Truth

Scripture Reading: John 8:32 – "Then you will know the truth, and the truth will set you free."

Reflection:

- How do I discern truth in an age of propaganda and misinformation?
- Have I allowed my political beliefs to shape my faith more than my faith has shaped my beliefs?

Additional Scripture Readings:

- Proverbs 3:5-6 – "Trust in the Lord with all your heart and lean not on your own understanding."

- Ephesians 6:14 – "Stand firm then, with the belt of truth buckled around your waist."

Prayer Focus:

Ask God for wisdom and discernment to recognize truth, even when it challenges your own assumptions.

Journal Section:

- Write down a recent situation where you struggled to discern truth. How did you respond? How can you seek God's wisdom in such situations?

Action Step:

Make a commitment this week to fact-check news sources and political narratives before forming strong opinions.

Week 2: Rejecting the Spirit of Fear

Scripture Reading: 2 Timothy 1:7 – "For God gave us a spirit not of fear but of power and love and self-control."

Reflection:

- What fears drive my political or ideological beliefs?

- Am I making decisions based on fear or on faith?

Additional Scripture Readings:

- Isaiah 41:10 – "So do not fear, for I am with you; do not be dismayed, for I am your God."

- Psalm 34:4 – "I sought the Lord, and he answered me; he delivered me from all my fears."

Prayer Focus:

Pray against fear-driven decision-making and ask for courage to stand in faith, not anxiety.

Journal Section:

- Reflect on a time when fear influenced your decision-making. How did it affect your actions and relationships?

Action Step:

This week, whenever you feel fear rising regarding cultural or political issues, take a moment to pause, pray, and seek God's peace.

Week 3: The Dangers of Dehumanization

Scripture Reading: Genesis 1:27 – "So God created mankind in his own image, in the image of God he created them; male and female he created them."

Reflection:

- Do I see those with different political views as fellow image-bearers of God?

- How can I extend grace to those with whom I deeply disagree?

Additional Scripture Readings:

- Matthew 5:44 – "But I tell you, love your enemies and pray for those who persecute you."

- Colossians 3:12-13 – "Therefore, as God's chosen people, holy and dearly loved, clothe yourselves with compassion, kindness, humility, gentleness and patience."

Prayer Focus:

Ask God to soften your heart toward those with opposing beliefs and to help you view them through His eyes.

Journal Section:

- Write about a recent interaction with someone who held an opposing viewpoint. How did you respond? What would you do differently in light of Scripture?

Action Step:

Engage in a conversation with someone who has a different perspective. Listen with the intent to understand, not to argue.

Week 4: Breaking Free from Strongholds

Scripture Reading: 2 Corinthians 10:4-5 – "The weapons we fight with are not the weapons of the world. On the contrary, they have divine power to demolish strongholds."

Reflection:

- What ideological strongholds have taken root in my heart?

- How can I allow God to renew my mind and free me from unhealthy attachments to political identities?

Additional Scripture Readings:

- Romans 12:2 – "Do not conform to the pattern of this world, but be transformed by the renewing of your mind."
- Psalm 139:23-24 – "Search me, God, and know my heart; test me and know my anxious thoughts."

Prayer Focus:

Pray for spiritual breakthrough, asking God to help you replace any ungodly strongholds with His truth.

Journal Section:

- Write down an area where you have felt emotionally or ideologically trapped. Surrender it to God in prayer, asking for His guidance and transformation.

Action Step:

Fast from social media or news for a day and use that time to meditate on God's Word.

Week 5: The Call to Reconciliation

Scripture Reading: Matthew 5:9 – "Blessed are the peacemakers, for they will be called children of God."

Reflection:

- Have I contributed to division rather than reconciliation?
- How can I become a bridge-builder in my family, church, or community?

Additional Scripture Readings:

- Ephesians 4:31-32 – "Get rid of all bitterness, rage and anger... Be kind and compassionate to one another."
- James 1:19 – "Everyone should be quick to listen, slow to speak and slow to become angry."

Prayer Focus:

Ask God to use you as an agent of peace and reconciliation, even when it is difficult.

Journal Section:

- Write a prayer asking God to show you ways to promote peace in your community and relationships.

Action Step:

Reach out to someone from the "other side" of the political spectrum and express a desire for unity despite differences.

Final Thought & Commitment

As followers of Christ, our highest allegiance is not to any political party but to God's Kingdom. Radicalization distorts our ability to love our neighbors and seek justice with humility. This week, commit to:

- Seeking truth above personal bias.
- Extending grace to those who disagree with you.
- Acting in love and wisdom rather than fear and hostility.

Journal Reflection:

- What key lesson has stood out to you in this devotional?
- How will you apply these biblical principles in your daily life?

May God strengthen you as you pursue truth, peace, and reconciliation in a divided world.

APPENDIX II

Inspirational Workbook & Reflective Guide

Strongholds! Breaking the Radicalization of Right & Left America

A Guided Journey of Self-Reflection & Growth

Ideological polarization has become one of the defining issues of our time. The way we engage with media, politics, and social discourse is increasingly shaped by echo chambers, emotional rhetoric, and tribal allegiances. This workbook is designed to help individuals critically examine their perspectives, challenge biases, and foster constructive dialogue, using wisdom from historical figures, philosophers, and thought leaders. Each section provides quotes, reflection questions, journaling prompts, and action steps to encourage deeper thinking and meaningful engagement with complex issues.

Week 1: Seeking Truth Beyond Bias

Quote:

"The greatest enemy of knowledge is not ignorance, it is the illusion of knowledge." – Daniel J. Boorstin

Reflection:

- Where do I get my information, and how do I verify its accuracy?

- Have I dismissed facts or perspectives because they challenge my beliefs?

Guided Insight:

True knowledge requires intellectual humility—the ability to recognize that we may not have all the answers. Developing a growth mindset allows us to be open to new ideas and to examine issues more objectively.

Journal Section:

Write about a time when new information changed your perspective on an issue. How did you react, and what did you learn from the experience?

Action Step:

Commit to engaging with one reputable source that presents an opposing viewpoint this week. Reflect on how it challenges or informs your thinking.

Week 2: Understanding Fear & Emotional Influence

Quote:

"Fear is the path to the dark side. Fear leads to anger, anger leads to hate, hate leads to suffering." – Yoda

Reflection:

- How does fear influence my opinions or reactions to political or social issues?
- Have I allowed emotions to override critical thinking?

Guided Insight:

Fear is a powerful force in shaping ideology. Propaganda and manipulative rhetoric often appeal to emotions to drive people toward extreme viewpoints. Recognizing these tactics can help us resist manipulation.

Journal Section:

Describe a situation where fear influenced your decision-making. How can you respond more rationally in the future?

Action Step:

The next time you feel a strong emotional reaction to an issue, pause and ask: *What facts support this emotion? Am I reacting or responding?*

Week 3: Avoiding Dehumanization & Tribalism

Quote:
"We are all human beings, and our nationality is simply an accident of birth." – Voltaire

Reflection:

- Do I view people with opposing views as my enemy?
- How can I engage with ideological opponents respectfully?

Guided Insight:

Radicalization often begins with dehumanization—
reducing individuals to labels rather than recognizing them
as complex human beings. Rebuilding empathy is key to
fostering a more constructive society.

Journal Section:

Think of a person whose views strongly oppose yours.
What might have shaped their beliefs? How can you
engage with them constructively?

Action Step:

Engage in a respectful conversation with someone who
has different views. Listen with curiosity rather than
defensiveness.

Week 4: Challenging Strongholds of Thought

Quote:

"A mind is like a parachute. It doesn't work if it is not open." –
Frank Zappa

Reflection:

- Have I ever changed my mind on a major issue?
  What led to that change?
- What strong opinions do I hold that I have never
  critically examined?

Guided Insight:

Ideological strongholds form when we stop questioning our beliefs. Being willing to change is a strength, not a weakness.

Journal Section:

Identify an issue you feel strongly about. Research a counterargument and write down any points that challenge your perspective.

Action Step:

Practice steel manning—the act of presenting the strongest possible version of an opposing viewpoint before refuting it.

Week 5: The Power of Dialogue & Civil Discourse

Quote:

"We have two ears and one mouth so that we can listen twice as much as we speak." – Epictetus

Reflection:

- Do I listen to understand or just to respond?
- How can I improve my communication in difficult conversations?

Guided Insight:

Engaging in civil discourse requires patience, listening, and a willingness to be wrong. True dialogue seeks to understand before debating.

Journal Section:

Write about a recent conversation where you struggled to listen. How could you have handled it differently?

Action Step:

In your next discussion, summarize the other person's argument before presenting your own. This ensures understanding and mutual respect.

Final Thought & Commitment

Breaking free from ideological radicalization requires continuous reflection and an openness to growth. Commit to lifelong learning and curiosity.

Final Journal Reflection:

- What was the most valuable lesson from this workbook?
- How will you continue practicing open-mindedness and critical thinking?

May your journey toward understanding lead to greater wisdom, balance, and clarity.

About the Author

Eric J. Freeman, PhD (Doctor of Philosophy in Homiletics and Social Ethics, Anderson University), Master of Arts in Religion (Theological Ethics, Lutheran Theological Southern Seminary), Bachelor of Science in Business Administration (Finance, University of Florida), is a scholar, author, and community leader dedicated to fostering critical thinking, ethical discourse, and interdisciplinary research. As the founder of *The Freeman Institute for Integrative Research*, he examines political polarization and social division through multiple academic lenses. His work integrates historical analysis, political theory, and sociological research to encourage balanced, informed engagement with America's deepening ideological divides. Dr. Freeman has advised civic and faith-based organizations on promoting constructive dialogue across political differences, and his methodologies for addressing extremism have been implemented in community forums throughout the Southeast. His lifelong mission is to empower individuals to navigate complex social landscapes with integrity, compassion, and a commitment to truth beyond partisan tribalism.

A PAMPHLET INITIATIVE OF

The
Freeman
Institute

FOR INTEGRATIVE RESEARCH

www.ingramcontent.com/pod-product-compliance
Lightning Source LLC
Chambersburg PA
CBHW021643270326
41931CB00008B/1152